Accrual Prepayments

REVISION WORKBOOK

Teresa Clarke FMAAT

ACCRUALS AND PREPAYMENTS

BY TERESA CLARKE FMAAT

CONTENTS:

Chapter 1	Introduction
Chapter 2	Exam Style Questions
Chapter 3	Practice Tasks with Worked Answers
Chapter 4	Advanced Tasks
Chapter 5	Practice, Practice, Practice
Chapter 6	Answers
Chapter 7	Quiz

WORKBOOK

Chapter 1 - Introduction

I have written this workbook to assist students who are studying bookkeeping or accountancy. It is particularly relevant for the AAT Level 3 Advanced Bookkeeping and Level 3 Advanced Synoptic units. It is not designed as a teaching tool but as a revision workbook. I hope it will help you to consolidate your studies so that you can become more confident with this subject and enable you to feel more comfortable with those tricky exam questions.

Accruals and prepayments are an essential element of AAT Level 3 Advanced Bookkeeping studies and the AAT Level 3 Advanced Synoptic exam, as well as other accounting qualifications such as A Level Accounting, ICB and ACCA qualifications.

Adjustments for accruals and prepayments are applied in real life and most businesses will apply adjustments for these at the end of their financial or accounting year in order to create accurate accounting records.

The accruals concept is a principle of accounting which requires the recording of income when it is earned and not when it is received; and the recording of expenses when they are incurred and not when they are paid for. Some studies will require you to explain the accruals concept, so I will try to help with that too.

Accrued expenses are expenses which have been incurred but have not yet been paid for. This means that we have used the expense, such as the electricity, but not yet paid for it.

Prepaid expenses are payments we have made for expenses but not yet incurred. This means that we have paid for an expense, such as insurance, in advance.

Accrued expenses become liabilities as they are owed by the business and prepaid expenses become assets because they have been paid in advance.

Accrued income is income which has been earned but not yet received. This means that the business is still owed some income for the period. This becomes an asset as it is owed to the business.

Prepaid income is income which has been received but not yet earned. This means that we have been paid for something that is not yet due. This becomes a liability as it is owed back to the customer until due.

I will explain the logic behind accruals and prepayments. This will help you to work through the activities in this workbook.

The accruals concept which is also known as the matching concept means that all income and expenses must be matched to the year in which they were incurred and not when money is received or paid. It is a good idea to practice writing down the definition of the accruals concept in your own words, as you might be asked to do this in a written part of an exam.

Tip: Accrued means owed, so accrued expenses are owed expenses and accrued income is owed income.

The DEAD CLIC rules can be applied to accruals and prepayments and I will be referring to these. Here is a reminder of this rule.

Debits increase
Expenses
Assets
Drawings

Credits increase
Liabilities
Income
Capital

It can be confusing when dealing with accrued expenses and prepaid expenses and then accrued income and prepaid income so we will look at these separately.

Remember:

The statement of profit and loss contains the income and expenses of the past financial year. Income and expense accounts are transferred to the statement of profit and loss at the end of the year. I will refer to this as the SoPL in the ledgers.

The statement of financial position contains assets and liabilities at a particular date, usually the last day of the financial year. This is a snapshot of the business at that date. Assets and liabilities are transferred to the statement of financial position at the end of the year and are carried down into the next financial year. You will see that these are showed with a bal c/d and bal b/d in the ledgers.

You will need to remember which statement the income, expenses, assets and liabilities are transferred to, so it is a good time to write down some notes. This might help.

SoPL – Income and Expenses
SoFP – Assets and Liabilities carried forward to the next year.

<u>Hint:</u> Make brief notes as you work through the book to help with the tasks later.

As we begin to work through some examples, we will work through some examples of accrued expenses and prepaid expenses first.

Accrued Expenses

The business rents a warehouse for storage of its finished goods. The rent expense for the warehouse is £1,000 per month. This means that the business must enter £12,000 as the expense for the year. This is 12 months of rent at £1,000 per month which is £12,000. I know you will agree that makes perfect sense.

However, the business has only paid £11,000 by the end of the financial year.

The business has used the warehouse for 12 months so incurred the rental expense for those 12 months. The amount to be entered into the accounting records for this expense should be £12,000. This is our warehouse rent expense incurred for the year. However, we have only paid £11,000 from the bank this year. The final £1,000 needs to be added to the warehouse rent expense account as a debit because this is an expense according to DEAD CLIC. And it needs to be added as a credit of £1,000 in the accrued expenses account because it is still owed at the end of the financial year.

Hint: Think of this as being similar to a trade payable, so a liability and liabilities are a credit according to DEAD CLIC.

When the accounts are balanced, the warehouse rent account has a balance to transfer to the statement of profit and loss of £12,000 and the accrued expense account has a balance to carry down of £1,000.

The expense account is transferred to the trial balance as a debit because expenses are debits according to DEAD CLIC, and then this is transferred to the statement of profit and loss.

The accruals account is transferred to the trial balance as a credit because this was still owed by the business at the end of the financial year, so a liability. This is then entered into the statement of financial position as a liability because it was still owed.

We can see this in the ledger accounts below. Take your time to read through these to check that you understand where the entries come from.

Warehouse rent expenses

Debit	£	Credit	£
Bank	11,000		
Accrued expenses	1,000	Transfer to SoPL	12,000
	12,000		12,000

Accrued expenses

Debit	£	Credit	£
Bal c/d	1,000	Warehouse rent expenses	1,000
	1,000		1,000
		Bal b/d	1,000

Remember:
Expenses are a debit in DEAD CLIC.

Accrued expenses are a credit as they are a liability because they were unpaid at the end of the financial year.

Hint:
When entering the bal c/d and bal b/d: Cap on top. Boots on bottom. So the C of c/d is above the B of b/d.

Prepaid Expenses

The insurance for the delivery van is £1,600 for 12 months and we have paid £1,800 this year. We can see that we have paid more insurance that was due for the year. This represents a prepaid expense which is carried forward to next year. This is because £200 has already been paid towards next year's insurance.

Because the insurance for the year is £1,600, we need to reduce the total in the insurance expense account by £200 for this current year (£1,800 less £1,600).

The expense account has a balance on the debit side of £1,800. We adjust this expense account by crediting it with £200 and entering the prepayment as a debit in the prepaid expenses account to be carried forward into next year's expense account. It is a prepayment because it has been prepaid for next year. It is a debit because this is an asset to the business, something that we are overpaid at the end of the financial year.

When the accounts are balanced, the insurance expense account has a balance to transfer to the statement of profit and loss of £1,600 and the prepaid expenses account has a balance to carry down of £200. The insurance expense account shows the correct expense for the year and the prepayment is carried forward into next year.

The expense account is transferred to the trial balance as a debit because expenses are debits according to DEAD CLIC and is then transferred the statement of profit and loss.

The prepaid expenses account is transferred to the trial balance as a debit because this is an asset to the business and is carried forward to the next financial year. This is because the prepaid expenses are an asset to the business so a debit according to DEAD CLIC and an asset in the statement of financial position.

We can see these entries in the ledger accounts now. Take your time to read through and understand the entries.

Insurance expenses

Debit	£	Credit	£
Bank	1,800	Prepaid expenses	200
		Transfer to SoPL	1,600
	1,800		1,800

Prepaid expenses

Debit	£	Credit	£
Insurance expenses	200		
		Bal c/d	200
	200		200
Bal b/d	200		

Remember:

Expenses are a debit in DEAD CLIC.

Prepaid expenses are a debit as they are an asset because they were prepaid at the end of the financial year, so owed back to the business at that point.

Note:

For an accrual you are adding in the expenses which **should** be in the year.

For a prepayment you are taking out expenses which **should not** be in the year.

Accrued Income

The business rents out a small office at the back of the main building to a self-employed architect. The rental income for this office is £200 per month. The architect has used the office for the full 12 months and has paid £2,000 this year.

The total rental income earned from this office rental is 12 months at £200 which is £2,400 (£200 x 12 = £2,400). The architect has paid £2,000 by the end of the financial year so this means that the architect still owed the business £400 in rent at the end of the year. This is an accrued (or owed) income.

Remember: Accrued means owed, so accrued income is owed income or income that is still owed to the business.

We need to adjust the accounting records because this rental income was earned, even if it has not yet been paid. In order to adjust the accounting records, we need to accrue £400 to the rental income account by crediting it by £400. We credit the account because we are increasing the rental income account and income is a credit according to DEAD CLIC. And we create an accrued income account and debit this with £400.

The accrued income account is debited because the income is owed to the business, so this is a form of asset. <u>Note</u>: This is very similar to a trade receivable.

When the accounts are balanced, the rental income account has a balance to transfer to the statement of profit and loss of £2,400, which is the total rental income earned for the year. The accrued income has a balance to carry down of £400 because this was still owed to the business at the end of the financial year.

The income account is transferred to the trial balance as a credit because income is a credit according to DEAD CLIC and is then transferred to the statement of profit and loss. The accrued income account is transferred to the trial balance as a debit because this is an asset to the business and is then enter into the statement of financial position.

Remember:

Income and expense accounts are transferred to the statement of profit and loss – SoPL.

Assets and liabilities are carried down into the next financial year and entered in the statement of financial position – SOFP.

These entries are shown in the ledgers below. Take a few minutes to check through the entries to ensure that you understand them.

Rental income

Debit	£	Credit	£
		Bank	2,000
Transfer to SoPL	2,400	Accrued income	400
	2,400		2,400

Accrued income

Debit	£	Credit	£
Rental income	400		
		Bal c/d	400
	400		400
Bal b/d	400		

Prepaid Income

The business rents out a storeroom to a builder for £150 per month and the builder has paid £1,950 by the end of the financial year.

The rent for the storeroom for the 12 months is: £150 x 12 months = £1,800. This shows that the builder has overpaid or prepaid £150. £1,950 paid less £1,800 owed equals £150 overpaid.

We need to adjust the rental income account by reducing it or debiting it with £150. We are debiting the account because rental income is a credit, and we want to reduce this account by £150. We create a prepaid income account and credit this with £150 as this is income that has been overpaid by the builder and is therefore a liability to the business at the end of the year. Liabilities are credits.

When the accounts are balanced the rental income account will have a balance of £1,800 to take to the statement of profit and loss; and the accrued income account will have a credit balance of £150 carry down and this is entered into the statement of financial position.

We can see these entries in the ledger accounts. Check that you understand the entries before moving on. Make some notes that you think will help you later too.

Rental income

Debit	£	Credit	£
Prepaid income	150	Bank	1,950
Transfer to SoPL	1,800		
	1,950		1,950

Prepaid income

Debit	£	Credit	£
Bal c/d	150	Rental income	150
	150		150
		Bal b/d	150

Remember:

Income is a credit in DEAD CLIC.

Prepaid income is a credit as this is a liability because it was prepaid or overpaid to the business at the end of the year.

Notes:

Make some notes to help you with the tasks that follow. You might like to remember the entries for accruals and prepayments like this.

Debits   **Credits**
PE   PI
AI   AE

Try to think of some sentences that would help to remember these, or perhaps use colours to draw a diagram of them.

Chapter 2 - Exam Style Questions

We will look at some exam style questions now and how to approach them.

If you like steps for completing tasks you might like this method.

Step 1: Enter the reversal or balance brought down.
Step 2: Enter the payments made from the bank or into the bank.
Step 3: Calculate the adjustment and enter this into the ledger accounts.
Step 4: Balance the accounts.

These steps will work for all accrual and prepayment questions, so it might be a good idea to write these out now.

Example without a reversal or bal b/d:
Accounting records show bank payments for telephone expenses have been made during the year of £560.

Because we do not have a reversal for this question, we start at step 2. This is an actual figure so goes into the telephone expenses as a debit and the bank as a credit. This money has actually been paid from the bank for the expenses so will be entered first. The expense account entry is a debit because expenses are debits according to DEAD CLIC. The bank account is a credit entry because the asset account is being reduced with the payment from the account.

We are told that the amount paid only covered 10 months of the year and a telephone bill of £120 was received for the final 2 months after the end of the year.

This is step 3, the adjustment. As the telephone bill was received after the end of the year it has not been entered into the accounting records.

The telephone expense of £120 belongs to the year as the expense was incurred during that period, so we add this to the telephone expenses as a debit and credit the accrued expenses account. The expense account is increased with this amount with a debit entry because expenses are debits. The accrued expenses account is credited because accrued expenses are owed expenses, and these are liabilities.

The telephone expenses account now has a full 12 months of expenses in it. It has the £560 paid from the bank and the £120 accrual which totals as an expense for the year of £680.

When balanced, the telephone expenses account will have a balance to transfer of £680 and this will be transferred to the statement of profit and loss at the end of the financial year. The accrued expenses account will have a balance to carry down of £120 and this will be entered into the statement of financial position.

Telephone expenses

Debit	£	Credit	£
Bank	560		
Accrued expenses	120	Transfer to P & L	680
	680		680

Accrued expenses

Debit	£	Credit	£
		Telephone expenses	120
Bal c/d	120		
	120		120
		Bal b/d	120

Here is another example:

Bank payments for the motor expenses showed that we had paid £890 for the year ending 31 December 2018, but this included one month for January 2019 of £100.

There is no reversal or balance brought down so we can ignore step 1 and go straight to step 2.

The bank payments show that we paid £890 so this is entered into the motor expenses account as a debit and into the bank account as a credit.

Step 3 is the adjustment. January's £100 does not belong in this year, so we 'take it out' by crediting the motor expenses and debiting the prepaid expenses. We are credit the motor expenses because motor expenses are debits, and we want to reduce the balance. The prepayments are a debit because this represents money that has been paid in advance, an asset.

When we balance the accounts the motor expenses account shows a balance of £790 and the prepaid expenses account shows a balance of £100.

Look at these entries in the ledger accounts below and make sure that you understand them before moving on.

Motor expenses

Debit	£	Credit	£
Bank	890	Prepaid expenses	100
		Transfer to SoPL	790
	890		890

Prepaid expenses

Debit	£	Credit	£
Motor expenses	100		
		Bal c/d	100
	100		100
Bal b/d	100		

Opening Accruals

The opening accrual or the reversal is essentially the balance brought down from the previous period.

In order to reverse an accruals account, you enter a double entry from the accruals account to the new expense or income account.

If you have a telephone expenses accrual of £120 on the credit side of the accrued expenses account, you debit this account and credit the telephone expenses for the next year. This clears the accrued expenses account by transferring it into the next year's expense account.

Take time to draw up the accrued expense account first with the balance like this:

Accrued expenses

Debit	£	Credit	£
		Telephone expenses	120

Then you can complete the double entry to transfer this from the accrued expenses account into the telephone expenses for the next period.

Accrued expenses

Debit	£	Credit	£
Reversal to telephone exp	120	Telephone expenses	120

Telephone expenses

Debit	£	Credit	£
		Reversal of accrued expenses	120

This is very much like entering a bal c/d in the accrued expenses and a bal b/d in the telephone expenses account.

Opening Prepayments

The opening prepayment or the reversal is essentially the balance brought down from the previous period.

In order to reverse a prepaid expenses account, you enter a double entry from the prepaid expenses to the new expense account.

If you have a motor expenses prepayment of £100 in the debit side of prepaid expenses account, you credit this account and debit the motor expenses for the next year. This clears the prepaid expenses account by transferring it into the next year's expense account.

Take time to draw up the prepaid expense account first with the balance like this:

Prepaid expenses

Debit	£	Credit	£
Motor expenses	100		

Then you can complete the double entry to transfer this from the prepaid expenses account into the motor expenses for the next period.

Prepaid expenses

Debit	£	Credit	£
Motor expenses	100	**Reversal to motor expenses**	**100**

Motor expenses

Debit	£	Credit	£
Prepaid expenses reversal	**100**		

Chapter 3 – Practice Tasks With Worked Answers

Work through the following activities and check your answers with the worked answers to ensure that you understand before moving on.

The questions increase in difficulty as you work through the tasks, so ensure that you feel confident before moving on.

<u>Remember</u>: Use the steps to approach each question.
Step 1: Enter the reversal or balance brought down from the previous period.
Step 2: Enter the bank payment or receipt.
Step 3: Calculate and enter the adjustment for the prepayment or accrual.
Step 4: Balance the accounts.

Task 1

You are working on the accounts of a business with the year ended 31 March 2018.

The bank summary shows payments of electricity expenses during the year of £2,300.

Included in that figure is £200 for the month of April 2018.

Prepare the electricity expense ledger account and the prepaid expenses ledger account. Balance the accounts with the appropriate bal c/d or transfer to the SoPL.

Electricity expenses

Debit	£	Credit	£

Prepaid expenses

Debit	£	Credit	£

Task 1 – worked answer

It is always a good idea to make a note of the year end – 31 March 2018.

Step 1 – There is no opening prepayment or accrual, so we can ignore this step.

The bank summary shows payments of electricity expenses during the year of £2,300.

Step 2 - This information tells you that these payments were made so must be entered into the relevant T accounts:
Payment is made from the bank. The bank is an asset, so if we reduce this, we need to credit this account. Even if the bank ledger account is not required as part of the task, it is always a good idea to draw this to ensure that your entries are on the correct sides.
Electricity expenses are expenses, so these are a debit in the electricity expenses ledger. (2)

Included in that figure is £200 for the month of April 2018.

Step 3 - This tells us that included in the amount paid some of this related to the month of April 2018. We can see that we are working on the accounts to March 2018, so the April payment does not belong in this year but is a prepaid expense for the following year. This is taken out of the current year and entered into the prepaid expenses account. As we are reducing the expenses for this year, we credit the expenses account.

The prepaid expenses account is debited as this is an asset to the business and this will be carried forward into the next accounting period. (3)

Prepare the electricity expense ledger account and the prepayments ledger account.

You can see that we were asked to prepare the electricity expense account, but it is easier to draw up all the ledgers until you become more comfortable with the subject.

Step 4 requires you to balance the accounts.

Remember: Income and expenses are transferred to the statement of profit and loss. Assets and liabilities are carried forward to the next accounting period.

In this question, electricity expenses are expenses and transferred to the statement of profit and loss. The prepaid expense account is an asset and carried down into the next accounting period. (4)

Electricity expenses

Debit	£	Credit	£
Bank (2)	2,300	Prepaid expenses (3)	200
		Transfer to SoPL (4)	2,100
	2,300		2,300

Bank

Debit	£	Credit	£
		Electricity expenses (2)	2,300
Bal c/d (4)	2,300		
	2,300		2,300
		Bal b/d (4)	2,300

Note: The bank account would probably have many other entries. It was not part of the task, but I have included it because it is a good way to check that you have entered your transactions on the correct sides.

Prepaid expenses

Debit	£	Credit	£
Electricity expenses (3)	200		
		Bal c/d (4)	200
	200		200
Bal b/d (4)	200		

Task 2

You are working on the accounts for the year ended 31 December 2019.

The bank summary shows payments of motor expenses during the year of £8,500.

Included in that figure is £500 for motor expenses prepaid for January and February 2020.

Prepare the motor expense ledger account and the prepaid expenses ledger account. Balance the accounts showing the appropriate bal b/d or transfer to the SoPL.

Remember: Make a note of the year end as you will need this for the adjustment in step 3.

Step 1: There is no balance to bring down from the previous period, so no reversal to enter.

Step 2: Enter the payments made from the bank into the bank ledger account and expense ledger account. *Remember that you may only be given one ledger account to complete, but it is always best to draw up all the relevant accounts.*

Step 3: Calculate the adjustment and enter the prepaid expenses into the expense ledger account and the prepaid expenses ledger account.

Step 4: Balance the accounts by transferring the balance to the statement of profit and loss or bal b/d.

Motor expenses

Debit	£	Credit	£

Prepaid expenses

Debit	£	Credit	£

Task 2 – worked answer

The year-end date is 31 December 2019.

Step 1: There is no balance to bring forward as a reversal.

Step 2 – The actual amount paid from the bank is £8,500 so this is entered into the bank ledger account and motor expenses ledger account. (2)

Step 3 – The bank payment of £500 relates to the months of January and February 2020 which are after the end of the year, so this is a prepaid expense and is entered into the motor expenses ledger account as a credit and prepaid expenses account as a debit. (3)

Step 4 – Balance the accounts and transfer the expenses to the SoPL and carry down the prepaid expenses to the next financial year. (4)

Motor expenses

Debit	£	Credit	£
Bank (2)	8,500	Prepaid expenses (3)	500
		Transfer to SoPL (4)	8,000
	8,500		8,500

Bank

Debit	£	Credit	£
		Motor expenses (2)	8,500

Note: The bank has only been included here to check that the transactions are entered on the correct sides.

Prepaid expenses

Debit	£	Credit	£
Motor expenses (3)	500		
		Bal c/d (4)	500
	500		500
Bal b/d (4)	500		

Task 3

You are working on the accounts for the year ended 31 October 2019.

The bank summary shows payments of office expenses during the year of £2,300.

Included in that figure is £100 for prepaid office rent for November 2019.

Prepare the office expense ledger account and the prepaid expenses ledger account, balancing the accounts off appropriately.

Office expenses

Debit	£	Credit	£

Prepaid expenses

Debit	£	Credit	£

Task 3 – answer

You are working on the accounts for the year ended **31 October 2019**.

Step 1 – There is no balance brought forward so we can ignore this step.

The **bank** summary shows payments of office expenses during the year of **£2,300**. **(2)**

Included in that figure is **£100** for **prepaid** office rent for November 2019. **(3)**

Prepare the **office expense ledger account** and the **prepaid expenses ledger account**.

We balance off the accounts with the office expenses being transferred to the statement of profit and loss and the prepaid expenses carried down into the next financial period. **(4)**

Office expenses

Debit	£	Credit	£
Bank (2)	2,300	Prepaid expenses (3)	100
		Transfer to SoPL (4)	2,200
	2,300		2,300

Prepaid expenses

Debit	£	Credit	£
Office expenses (3)	100		
		Bal c/d (4)	100
	100		100
Bal b/d (4)	100		

Task 4

You are working on the accounts for the year ended 31 December 2019.

The bank summary shows payments of electricity expenses during the year of £2,800 covering the months of January 2019 to November 2019.

An electricity bill for £190 for the month of December 2019 was received after the year end.

Prepare the electricity expense ledger account and the accrued expenses ledger account, balancing the accounts off appropriately.

Electricity expenses

Debit	£	Credit	£

Accrued expenses

Debit	£	Credit	£

Task 4 – worked answer

You are working on the accounts for the year ended 31 December 2019.

Make a note of the year end – 31 December 2019.

Step 1 – There is no opening balance or reversal so we can ignore this step.

The bank summary shows payments of electricity expenses during the year of £2,800 covering the months of January 2019 to November 2019.

Step 2 – Enter the electricity expenses paid from the bank into the bank and expense ledger accounts. (2)

An electricity bill for £190 for the month of December 2019 was received after the year end.

Step 3 – The electricity expense for December has been incurred, which means that the electricity has been used. However, this was not paid for by the end of the year, so this needs to be added into the expense account for the year. This is an accrual or accrued expense. We need to enter this into the expense ledger account so that the full 12 months of expenses are shown and into the accrued expenses ledger account as an 'owed expense'. (3)

Prepare the electricity expense ledger account and the accrued expenses ledger account, balancing off appropriately.

Remember to draw up all the accounts that are relevant to help you with this question.

Electricity expenses

Debit	£	Credit	£
Bank (2)	2,800		
Accrued expenses (3)	190	Transfer to SoPL (4)	2,990
	2,990		2,990

The bank account is shown here but was not required in the task. It is helpful to draw up any accounts that assist you to complete a task. As the money came out of the bank and into the expenses account for step 2, I have drawn this to show the credit entry in the bank and the debit entry in the electricity expenses.

Bank

Debit	£	Credit	£
		Electricity expenses (2)	2,800

Accrued expenses

Debit	£	Credit	£
		Electricity expenses (3)	190
Bal c/d (4)	190		
	190		190
		Bal b/d (4)	190

Task 5

You are working on the accounts for the year ended 31 March 2019.

The bank summary shows payments of motor expenses during the year of £6,700.

An invoice for motor repairs of £320 was received in June 2019 for repairs carried out in February 2019.

Prepare the motor expense ledger account and the accrued expenses ledger account, balancing them off appropriately.

Motor expenses

Debit	£	Credit	£

Accrued expenses

Debit	£	Credit	£

Task 5 – worked answer

You are working on the accounts for the year ended 31 March 2019.

The year end is 31 March 2019

Step 1 – There is no reversal or opening balance, so we can ignore this step.

The bank summary shows payments of motor expenses during the year of £6,700.

Step 2 – Enter the expenses actually paid from the bank into the bank and motor expenses ledger accounts. (2)

An invoice for motor repairs of £320 was received in June 2019 for repairs carried out in February 2019.

Step 3 – This invoice was received in June, which was after the end of the year, but the expense was incurred or spent in February, which was before the end of the year. We need to enter expenses when they are incurred and not when paid, so this is entered into the motor expenses ledger account as the expense relates to this period, and into the accrued expenses ledger account because it was an 'owed expense' at the end of the year. (3)

Step 4 – Balance the accounts, remembering that expenses to the SoPL and liabilities are carried down into the next period. (4)

Prepare the motor expense ledger account and the accrued expenses ledger account.

We enter the transactions using the steps, drawing the bank account in our notes to help guide us through the double entries.

Motor expenses

Debit	£	Credit	£
Bank (2)	6,700		
Accrued expenses (3)	320	Transfer to SoPL (4)	7,020
	7,020		7,020

Bank

Debit	£	Credit	£
		Motor expenses (2)	6,700

Accrued expenses

Debit	£	Credit	£
		Motor expenses (3)	320
Bal c/d (4)	320		
	320		320
		Bal b/d (4)	320

Task 6

You are working on the accounts for the year ended 31 December 2019.

The bank summary shows payments of rent expenses during the year of £2,200 covering the months from January 2019 to the end of November 2019.

Prepare the rent expense ledger account and the accrued expenses ledger account, balancing off the accounts appropriately.

Rent expenses

Debit	£	Credit	£

Accrued expenses

Debit	£	Credit	£

Task 6 – worked answer

You are working on the accounts for the year ended **31 December 2019**.

Step 1 – There is no opening balance or reversal, so we can ignore this step.

Step 2 - The bank summary shows payments of rent expenses during the year of **£2,200** covering the months from **January 2019 to the end of November 2019 (11 months). (2)**

Step 3 - The payments have only covered 11 months of rent, so a further month needs to be included to accurately show the rent expense for the full 12 months of expense incurred.

Workings: £2,200 / 11 months = £200 per month. £200 needs to be added to the rent expense account for December's rent and added to the accrued expense account because it was still owed at the end of the year. (2)

Prepare the **rent expense ledger account** and the **accrued expenses ledger account**.

Rent expenses

Debit	£	Credit	£
Bank (2)	2,200		
Accrued expenses (3)	200	Transfer to SoPL (4)	2,400
	2,400		2,400

Accrued expenses

Debit	£	Credit	£
		Rent expenses (3)	200
Bal c/d (4)	200		
	200		200
		Bal b/d (4)	200

Task 7

You are working on the accounts for the year ended 30 June 2018.

Bank payments of £1,600 have been made for admin expenses during the year.

An invoice for paper of £30 purchased in May 2018 was received and paid for in July 2018.

Prepare the admin expenses ledger account and the accrued expense or prepaid expense account for the year.

Note: In this question you need to decide whether this is a prepaid expense or an accrued expense.

Admin expenses

Debit	£	Credit	£

....

Debit	£	Credit	£

Task 7 - answer

You are working on the accounts for the year ended **30 June 2018.**

Step 1 – There is no opening balance or reversal, so you can ignore this step.

Step 2 - Bank payments of £1,600 have been made for **admin expenses** during the year. **(2)**

Step 3 - An invoice for paper of **£30** purchased in **May 2018** was received and paid for in **July 2018. This expense was incurred or spent before the end of the year, but not paid for until after the year, so needs to be included with the year's expenses as an accrued or owed expense. (3)**

Prepare the **admin expenses ledger account** and the **accrued expense** or **prepaid expense** account for the year. **As the expense was incurred within the year, but not paid for at the year-end, this was still owed at the end of the year so this an accrued expense.**

Step 4 – Remember to balance the accounts with the expenses going to the SoPL and the accrued expenses carried down into the next financial period.

Note: Exam questions will usually require you to work out whether it is an accrued expense, prepaid expense, accrued income or prepaid expense, so make sure that you understand this before moving on.

Admin expenses

Debit	£	Credit	£
Bank (2)	1,600		
Accrued expenses (3)	30		
		Transfer to SoPL (4)	1,630
	1,630		1,630

Accrued expenses

Debit	£	Credit	£
		Admin expenses (3)	30
Bal c/d (4)	30		
	30		30
		Bal b/d (4)	30

Task 9

You are working on the accounts for the year ended 31 March 2018.

The bank summary shows receipts of rental income during the year of £15,600.

The rent due for the year is £13,200.

Prepare the rental income account for the year and the prepaid income account for the year, balancing off the accounts appropriately.

Note: This is an income account, so you need to think about DEAD CLIC. Income is a credit.

Remember: Prepaid income is a liability because it is owed back to the payer. Accrued income is an asset because it is owed to the business by the payer.

Rental income

Debit	£	Credit	£

Prepaid income

Debit	£	Credit	£

Task 9 – worked answer

You are working on the accounts for the year ended **31 March 2018.**

Step 1 – There is no opening balance or reversal, so we can ignore this step.

Step 2 - The **bank summary shows receipts** of rental income during the year of **£15,600**. We note that this is an income account.

Step 3 - The rent due for the year is **£13,200. This is the amount of rent due to the business for the full year, 12 months. We need to calculate the amount of over or underpayment of rent. The rent due was £13,200, but we have been paid £15,600. This means that the rent income has been overpaid or paid in advance by £2,400 (£15,600 - £13,200). We need to adjust for this overpayment or prepaid income.**

Step 4 - Prepare the rental income account for the year and the prepaid income account for the year, balancing off the accounts appropriately. **Income and expenses are transferred to the statement of profit and loss and accruals and prepayments are carried forward into the next financial period.**

Workings:
2. **The bank payment was received, so the bank was debited and the rental income account credited.**
3. **The rent due for the year was £13,200, so the difference is the prepaid income, because the amount going to the SoPL needs to be the full year's rent due and no more.**
4. **Balance off the income account with the balancing figure going to the statement of profit and loss. Balance off the prepaid income account by carrying it down into the next period.**

Rental income

Debit	£	Credit	£
Prepaid income (3)	2,400	Bank (2)	15,600
Transfer to SoPL (4)	13,200		
	15,600		15,600

Prepaid income

Debit	£	Credit	£
		Rental income (3)	2,400
Bal c/d (4)	2,400		
	2,400		2,400
		Bal b/d (4)	2,400

Task 10

You are working on the accounts for the year ended 31 March 2019.

You are told that the rental income had an opening prepayment of £750.

The bank summary shows receipts of rental income during the year of £6,500.

The rent due is £500 per calendar month.

Prepare the rental income account for the year and the appropriate prepaid income or accrued income accounts, balancing them off appropriately.

<u>Note</u>: This question has an opening prepayment – Step 1.

<u>Note</u>: You are required to work out in step 3 whether it is an accrual or prepayment.

Rental income

Debit	£	Credit	£

....

Debit	£	Credit	£

Task 10 – worked answer

You are working on the accounts for the year ended **31 March 2019**.

Step 1 -You are told that the rental income had an **opening prepayment of £750**. This is an income account, so the opening prepayment is a liability to the business as represents an over-payment by the customer at this point, so this is a credit. Think about the table we looked at earlier in the workbook (page 14).

Debits	Credits
PE	PI
AI	AE

This will help you to work out which side the reversal goes in the income ledger.

Step 2 - The **bank summary shows receipts** of rental income during the year of **£6,500**.

Step 3 - The rent due is £500 per calendar month. The adjustment needs to be calculated based on the rental income due for the year.

Step 4 -Prepare the rental income account for the year and the appropriate prepaid income or accrued income accounts, balancing them off appropriately.

Hint: This task has more details, so make sure you work through it step by step.

Workings:
The prepaid income was a credit (liability), so the double entry would be to debit the prepaid income and credit the rental income. (step 1)
Bank payment was received, so the bank was debited and the rental income credited. (step 2)
The rent for the year was £500 x 12 = £6,000 so this needs to be the amount to transfer to the SoPL. The balancing amount is the prepaid income.

Rental income

Debit	£	Credit	£
Prepaid income (3)	1,250	Prepaid income reversal (1)	750
Transfer to SoPL (4)	6,000	Bank (2)	6,500
	7,250		7,250

Prepaid income

Debit	£	Credit	£
		Rental income (3)	1,250
Bal c/d (4)	1,250		
	1,250		1,250
		Bal b/d (4)	1,250

Take your time to understand the entries for this one, as it was a different style of question. You were given the amount to transfer to the statement of profit and loss, the income for the year. The balancing amount of £1,250 was the income overpaid, so the prepaid income.

Task 11

You are working on the accounts for the year ended 31 December 2019.

You are told that the rental income had an opening accrual of £300.

The bank summary shows receipts of rental income during the year of £7,800.

The rent due is £600 per calendar month.

Prepare the rental income account for the year and the relevant prepaid income or accrued income account, balancing them off appropriately.

<u>Remember</u>: There is an opening accrual in this task, which is your step 1.

Rental income

Debit	£	Credit	£

....

Debit	£	Credit	£

Task 11 – worked answer

You are working on the accounts for the year ended **31 December 2019.**

Step 1 - You are told that the **rental income** had an **opening accrual** of **£300. This is an income account, so the accrual is reversed from the accrued income account into the rental income account by crediting the accrued income account to remove it and debiting it to the rental income account. (This is a debit in the rental income account because the money does not belong to this current year, but to the previous year). (1)**

Step 2 - The **bank summary shows receipts** of rental income during the year of **£7,800. This was the amount received, so this is debited to the bank account and credited to the rental income account. (2)**

Step 3 -The rent due is **£600** per calendar month. **We can calculate how much rent was due for the year by multiplying £600 by 12 months to get £7,200. This is the amount of rent which has been earned but not necessarily received yet and represents the rental income for the year in the statement of profit and loss. (3)**

Step 4 - Prepare the rental income account for the year and the relevant prepaid income or accrued income account, balancing them off appropriately. **(4)**

Remember that the balancing figure is the closing prepayment in the rental income account. (4)

Rental income

Debit	£	Credit	£
Opening accrual/reversal (1)	300	Bank (2)	7,800
Transfer to SoPL (4)	7,200		
Prepaid income (3)	300		
	7,800		7,800

Note that the balancing figure in the rental income account represents overpaid rent, so prepaid income.

Prepaid income

Debit	£	Credit	£
		Rental income (3)	300
Bal c/d (4)	300		
			300
		Bal b/d (4)	300

Note that the entry in the prepaid income is a credit because this is a liability at the year end. This is because the rental income was overpaid, and this was owed back to the payer at that point. It will be carried forward into the next accounting period when it will be due.

Task 12

You are working on the accounts for the year ended 31 August 2019.

You are told that the office expenses account has an opening accrual of £78 for some stationery which was used during the previous year but not paid for until December 2018.

The bank summary shows payments of office expenses were made during the year of £3,850.

On 2 November 2019, an invoice for £50 was received for office stationery received and used in August 2019.

Prepare the office expenses account for the year and the correct accruals or prepayments account, balancing them off appropriately.

Office expenses

Debit	£	Credit	£

....

Debit	£	Credit	£

Task 12 – worked answer

You are working on the accounts for the year ended **31 August 2019. We note that the year of the account is from 1 September 2018 to 31 August 2019. It is always a good idea to write the start and end dates of the financial year, particularly if it is not January to December.**

Step 1 - You are told that the office expenses account has an **opening accrual of £78** for some stationery which was used during the previous year but not paid for until December 2018. **This is an opening balance for accrued expenses, so this is *owed back* to the previous year, therefore a credit entry in the accrued expenses account. When we move this, we debit the accrued expenses account and reverse this into the office expenses account as a credit. (1)**

Step 2 - The **bank** summary shows **payments** of office expenses were made during the year of **£3,850. This shows payments that were made during the year, so these are debited to the office expenses account and credited to the bank account. (2)**

Step 3 - On **2 November 2019** an invoice for **£50** is received for office stationery received and used in **August 2019. This invoice has been received for stationery used during the year, but payment was not made during the year.**

We need to account for this as the expense was incurred during the year, even though it was not paid for until after the year end. This amount is added or debited to the office expenses account and credited to the accruals or accrued expenses account because it was still owed at the end of the year. (3)

Step 4 - Prepare the office expenses account for the year and the correct accruals or prepayments account, balancing them off appropriately. **The office expenses account is balanced off and the balancing figure shows the total office expenses for the year, which is transferred to the statement of profit and loss. The accrued expenses account is balanced with a balanced carried down into the next financial year. (4)**

Office expenses

Debit	£	Credit	£
Bank (2)	3,850	Reversal of accrual (1)	78
Accrued expenses (3)	50	Transfer to SoPL (4)	3,822
	3,900		3,900

Accrued expenses

Debit	£	Credit	£
		Office expenses (3)	50
Bal c/d (4)	50		
	50		50
		Bal b/d (4)	50

Task 13

You are working on the accounts for the year ended 31 December 2019.

You are told that the motor expenses account has an opening prepayment of £400.

The bank summary shows payments of motor expenses during the year of £12,620.

Included in that figure is a payment for van insurance of £900, which covered the period from 1 March 2019 to 28 February 2020.

Prepare the motor expenses account and the correct accruals or prepayments account, balancing them off appropriately.

Motor expenses

Debit	£	Credit	£

....

Debit	£	Credit	£

Task 13 – worked answer

You are working on the accounts for the year ended 31 December 2019. **Note that the year of the accounts is 1 January 2019 to 31 December 2019.**

Step 1 - You are told that the motor expenses account has an opening prepayment of £400. **This amount was prepaid in the last year so is an opening prepayment for this year. It was an asset at the end of the last year, so was a debit in the prepaid expenses account. We reverse this by crediting the prepaid expenses account and debiting the motor expenses account. (1)**

Step 2 - The **bank** summary shows payments of motor expenses during the year of **£12,620. This was the amount paid from the bank so is debited to the motor expenses and credited to the bank account. (2)**

Step 3 - Included in that figure is a payment for van insurance of **£900**, which covered the period from **1 March 2019 to 28 February 2020.** This states that this amount was *included* in the amount paid but represents the period from 1 March 2019 to 28 February 2020.

We can see that the year we are working on ends on 31 December 2019, so the months of January 2020 and February 2020 are not part of the year. The amount paid for these months represents a prepayment for the next year. £900 / 12 months gives the monthly amount of £75 and the two months of January and February 2020 represent £150 of prepayment for the following year (£75 x 2). The motor expenses account is credited to *remove* it from the current year and debited to the prepaid expenses account as an asset to be carried forward into the next year. (3)

Step 4 - Prepare the motor expenses account and the correct accruals or prepayments account, balancing them off appropriately. **The balancing figure in the motor expenses account will be the amount of motor expenses for the year to be transferred to the statement of profit and loss. The balance in the prepaid expenses account is carried down into the next financial period. (4)**

Motor expenses

Debit	£	Credit	£
Prepayment reversal (1)	400	Prepaid expenses (3)	150
Bank (2)	12,620	Transfer to P & L (4)	12,870
	13,020		13,020

Prepaid expenses

Debit	£	Credit	£
Motor expenses (3)	150		
		Bal c/d (4)	150
	150		150
Bal b/d (4)	150		

Chapter 4 – Advanced Tasks

These questions are more complex. The answers are given at the end of the book.

Task 14

You are working on the accounts for a business with a year end of 31 March 2019.

You have been provided with the following information:

The balance on the admin expenses account at 1 April 2018 was £400. This represented a prepayment of admin expenses.

The balance on the motor expenses account at 1 April 2018 was £630. This represented an accrual of motor expenses.

Bank payments during the year were:
Admin expenses   £2,620
Motor expenses   £7,200

After the year end a purchase invoice for stationery was received but not paid for and this was for £82.

The motor expenses included a payment for motor insurance of £960 which covered the period from 1 February 2019 to 30 April 2019.

Calculate the total for admin expenses and motor expenses to be transferred to the statement of profit and loss for the year ended 31 March 2019.

Note: The task has not asked for the prepayments or accruals accounts, but you might find it useful to draw those up to check your entries.

Admin expenses

Debit	£	Credit	£

Motor expenses

Debit	£	Credit	£

....

Debit	£	Credit	£

....

Debit	£	Credit	£

Task 15

You are working on the accounts for a business with a year end of 31 December 2019.

You are given the following information:

Balances at 1 January 2019	£
Prepayment for advertising expenses	340
Accrual for rent expenses	600

The bank summary shows payments during the year of £3,600 for advertising expenses and £7,200 for rent expenses.

Included in the rent expenses paid is £600 for January 2020.

On 20 January 2020, an invoice for advertising expenses of £45 was received and paid for an advert placed in November 2019.

You are required to draw up the rent expenses and advertising expenses accounts showing clearly the amount to be transferred to the statement of profit and loss.

Note: The task does not require you to draw up the accruals or prepayments accounts, but you might find it useful to draw these to check that your entries are on the correct sides.

Rent expenses

Debit	£	Credit	£

Advertising expenses

Debit	£	Credit	£

....

Debit	£	Credit	£

....

Debit	£	Credit	£

Task 16

You have been asked to make the appropriate adjustments to the commission income account for the year to 31 August 2019.

You have been given the following information:

At 1 September 2018 there was an opening accrual of commission income to the value of £425.

The cash book shows receipts of commission income during the year of £8,750.

Commission of £730 for the month of August 2019 was received on 30 September 2019.

Complete the commission income account showing clearly the amount to be transferred to the statement of profit and loss. Complete the relevant accrued income or prepaid income account, balancing it off appropriately.

Commission income

Debit	£	Credit	£

....

Debit	£	Credit	£

Task 17

You are working on the accounts for the year ended 31 March 2019.

You have been given the following information:

Opening prepayment of rental income £900
Bank receipts for rental income £9,000
Rent income earned is £900 per month for the full 12 months.

Complete the rental income account for the year ended 31 March 2019 showing clearly the amount to be transferred to the statement of profit and loss. Complete the relevant accrued or prepaid income account, showing clearly the amount to be carried down.

Rent income

Debit	£	Credit	£

....

Debit	£	Credit	£

Task 18

Using your answers to task 17, complete the following statements:

The date for the opening prepayment of rental income is ....

The date for the closing accrual of rental income is ....

The total rental income for the year is ....
This is transferred to the statement of ....

An amount of £................ is transferred to the statement of .... as prepaid income/accrued income.

This is listed as a non-current asset/current asset/current liability.

Task 19

Below is an extract from the extended trial balance. Complete the table by transferring the totals to the correct column.

Note: The debits and credits will not balance as this is only an extract of the trial balance.

Account	£	Debit	Credit
Accrued income	310		
Discounts received	86		
Prepaid expenses	240		
Machinery at cost	20,400		
Accrued expenses	650		
Sales returns	370		
Prepaid income	680		
VAT owed to HMRC	12,644		

Task 20

This is the big one and likely to be more difficult than a question you might get in your exam!

You are working on the accounts for the year end 30 September 2019.

You have been provided with the following information:

Accrual of motor expenses at 1 October 2018	£535
Prepayment of telephone expenses at 1 October 2018	£120
Prepayment of rental income at 1 October 2018	£1,200
Bank payments of motor expenses during the year	£6,600
Bank payments of telephone expenses during the year	£1,400
Rental income received during the year	£15,600

You are given the following information for the year-end adjustments:

The bank payments of motor expenses included insurance for the quarter ended 30 November 2019 of £333.

After the year end an invoice of £240 for telephone expenses for the quarter ended 31 October 2019 was received and paid.

Rental income is £1,200 per month for the full 12 months.

You are required to prepare the motor expenses, telephone expenses and rental income accounts for the year ended 30 September clearly showing the amounts to be transferred to the statement of profit and loss.

Note: You might find it useful to draw up other accounts to help you with this task.

Motor expenses

Debit	£	Credit	£

Telephone expenses

Debit	£	Credit	£

Rental income

Debit	£	Credit	£

....

Debit	£	Credit	£

....

Debit	£	Credit	£

....

Debit	£	Credit	£

Chapter 5 – Practice, Practice, Practice

Task 21

You have been provided with the following information about a business with the year end of 31 March 2020.

The balance on the rent income account at the beginning of the financial year was £300 and this represented a prepayment of rental income.

The cashbook shows receipts of rental income during the year of £3,800.

Included in the payments received was amount of £300 covering the period from 1 February 2020 to 30 April 2020.

Calculate the rent income for the year ended 31 March 2020 to be transferred to the statement of profit and loss.

Answer _____

Hint: This task has not asked you to complete the rental income account, but it is always a good idea to do this. A blank T account is shown below for you to use.

Remember: Use the steps to ensure that you enter all the transactions.

Debit	£	Credit	£

Task 22

You are working on the accounts of a business with the year end of 30 June 2020.

You are told that there is an opening prepayment on the insurance expense account of £500.

Bank payments made during the year for insurance expenses totalled £5,800.

Included in those payments were the following:

Van insurance	1 August 2019 – 31 July 2020	£480
Lorry insurance	1 November 2019 – 31 October 2020	£1200

Complete the insurance account below, clearly showing the amount to be transferred to the statement of profit and loss.

<u>Note:</u> The task is not asking for a prepayment or accrual account, but you might find it useful to draw this too.

Insurance expenses

Debit	£	Credit	£

....

Debit	£	Credit	£

Task 23

TDJ Partnerships owns business premises and sublets one of its warehouses to another business for £120,000 a year. On the 1 January 2020 there was £20,000 of rent still owing. During the year ended 31 December 2020 £110,000 of rent payments were received.

Write up the rental income account for TDJ Partnership and the relevant accruals or prepayment account, balancing off the accounts appropriately.

Warehouse rent income

Debit	£	Credit	£

....

Debit	£	Credit	£

Task 24:

TYL Manufacturing have a year end of 31 December. During the year to 31 December 2020 the following electricity bills were received and paid.

January, February and March £380

April, May and June £450

July, August and September £410

Write up the electricity account for the year based on this information.

Hint: You will need to estimate electricity costs based on usage through the year.

Note: The task has not asked for the accruals or prepayments account, but you might like to draw this to help you complete the task correctly.

Electricity expenses

Debit	£	Credit	£

....

Debit	£	Credit	£

Task 25

Enter the figures below into the correct debit or credit columns of the extract from the trial balance.

Ledger Account	Ledger Balance £	Debit £	Credit £
Prepaid expenses	360		
Accrued income	500		
Accrued expenses	800		
Prepaid income	940		

Task 26

The year end of a business is 31 March 2021. The balance on the prepaid expenses account at the start of the year was £300 and this represented prepaid insurance. Bank payments of £970 were made during the year. Included in that amount was a payment of £450 for the quarter ended 30 April 2021.

Complete the following sentences:

The balance on the insurance expense account at the start of the year was £300

The adjustment at the end of the year on the insurance expense account was

£150 and this represented a *prepaid expense* / *accrued expense*.

The amount of insurance expenses to be transferred to the statement of profit and loss

at the end of the year is £1,120.

ACCRUALS AND PREPAYMENTS WORKBOOK

<u>Note</u>: The task does not require the T account to be completed, but you might find it useful to draw this to guide you through completing the sentences above.

....

Debit	£	Credit	£

Chapter 6 - Answers

Task 14 - worked answer

You are working on the accounts for a business with a year end of **31 March 2019**.

You have been provided with the following information:

Step 1 - The balance on the **admin expenses** account at **1 April 2018** was **£400**. This represented a **prepayment** of admin expenses.

Step 1 - The balance on the **motor expenses** account at **1 April 2018** was **£630**. This represented an **accrual** of motor expenses.

Step 2 - **Bank payments** during the year were:

Admin expenses £2,620

Motor expenses £7,200

Step 3 - **After the year end** a purchase invoice for **stationery** was received but not paid for and this was for **£82**. **This was received after the year end, so it was still owed at the end of the year. An owed expense is an accrued expense.**

Step 3 - The **motor expenses** included a payment for motor insurance of **£960** which covered the period from **1 February 2019 to 30 April 2019.** **The year end is 31 March 2019. The payment of £960 covers February, March and April 2019. April belongs in the next year, so this is a prepaid expense.**

Step 4 - Calculate the total for admin expenses and motor expenses to be transferred to the statement of profit and loss for the year ended 31 March 2019.

Admin expenses

Debit	£	Credit	£
Prepayment reversal (1)	400		
Bank (2)	2,620		
Accrued expenses (3)	82	Transfer to SoPL (4)	3,102
	3,102		3,102

Motor expenses

Debit	£	Credit	£
Bank (2)	7,200	Accrual reversal (1)	630
		Prepayments (W) (3)	320
		Transfer to SoPL (4)	6,250
	7,200		7,200

W = Prepaid motor expenses: £960 for 1 February to 30 April 2019. Two months belong within the year to 31 March 2019, and one does not belong. This payment has been made so one month needs to be deducted from the expenses as a prepayment for the following year.

£960 / 3 = £320 for one month.

Task 15 – worked answer

You are working on the accounts for a business with a year end of **31 December 2019**.

Step 1:
You are given the following information:

Balances at 1 January 2019	£
Prepayment for advertising expenses	**340**
Accrual for rent expenses	**600**

Step 2 - The bank summary shows payments during the year of **£3,600 for advertising expenses** and **£7,200 for rent expenses.**

Step 3 - **Included** in the **rent expenses paid** is **£600 for January 2020.**

Step 3 - On **20 January 2020** an invoice for **advertising expenses** of **£45 was received and paid** for an advert placed in **November 2019**.

Step 4 - You are required to draw up the rent expenses and advertising expenses accounts showing clearly the amount to be transferred to the statement of profit and loss.

Advertising expenses

Debit	£	Credit	£
Prepayment reversal (1)	340		
Bank (2)	3,600		
Accrued expenses (3)	45	Transfer to SoPL (4)	3,985
	3,985		3,985

Rent expenses

Debit	£	Credit	£
Bank (2)	7,200	Accruals reversal (1)	600
		Prepaid expenses (3)	600
		Transfer to SoPL (4)	6,000
	7,200		7,200

Task 16 - worked answer

You have been asked to make the appropriate adjustments to the **commission income** account for the year to **31 August 2019**.

You have been given the following information:

Step 1 - At **1 September 2018** there was an **opening accrual** of **commission income** to the value of **£425**.

Step 2 - The **cash book** shows **receipts of commission income** during the year of **£8,750**.

Step 3 - Commission of **£730** for the month of **August 2019** was **received on 30 September 2019.**

Step 4 - Complete the commission income account showing clearly the amount to be transferred to the statement of profit and loss. Complete the relevant accrued income or prepaid income account, balancing it off appropriately.

Commission income

Debit	£	Credit	£
Accrued income reversal (1)	425	Bank (cash book) (2)	8,750
Transfer to SoPL (4)	9,055	Accrued income (3)	730
	9,480		9,480

Accrued income

Debit	£	Credit	£
Commission income (3)	730		
		Bal c/d (4)	730
	730		730
Bal b/d (4)	730		

Task 17 - worked answer

You are working on the accounts for the year ended **31 March 2019.**

You have been given the following information:

Step 1 - Opening prepayment of rental income   £900
Step 2 - Bank receipts for rental income   £9,000
Step 3 - Rent income earned is £900 per month for the full 12 months.

Complete the rental income account for the year ended 31 March 2019 showing clearly the amount to be transferred to the statement of profit and loss. Complete the relevant accrued or prepaid income account, showing clearly the amount to be carried down.

Rent income

Debit	£	Credit	£
		Prepaid income reversal (1)	900
		Bank (2)	9,000
Transfer to SoPL (W) (4)	10,800	Accrued income (3)	900
	10,800		10,800

Accrued income

Debit	£	Credit	£
Rent income (3)	900		
		Bal c/d	900
	900		900
Bal b/d	900		

Workings: In this question we were given the rental income for the year of £900 per month x 12 months so the amount to be transferred to the statement of profit and loss is £900 x 12, which is £10,800. The account can then be balanced which shows accrued income of £900.

Task 18 answer

Using your answers to task 17, complete the following statements:

The date for the opening prepayment of rental income is **1 April 2018.**

The date for the closing accrual of rental income is **31 March 2019.**

The total rental income for the year is **£10,800.**

This is transferred to the statement of **profit and loss.**

An amount of £**900** is transferred to the statement of **financial position** as prepaid income/**accrued income**.

This is listed as a non-current asset/**current asset**/current liability.

Task 19 – worked answer

Below is an extract from the extended trial balance. Complete the table by transferring the totals to the correct column.

Note: The debits and credits will not balance as this is only an extract of the trial balance.

Account	£	Debit	Credit
Accrued income	310	<u>310</u>	
Discounts received	86		<u>86</u>
Prepaid expenses	240	<u>240</u>	
Machinery at cost	20,400	<u>20,400</u>	
Accrued expenses	650		<u>650</u>
Sales returns	370	<u>370</u>	
Prepaid income	680		<u>680</u>
VAT owed to HMRC	12,644		<u>12,644</u>

Explanations:

Accrued income is income that is owed to the business, a form of receivable, so an asset.

Discounts received are received by the business so are a form of income.

Prepaid expenses are payments made in advance for expenses not yet incurred, so these are an asset.

Machinery at cost is an asset because it is owned by the business.

Accrued expenses are owed by the business for expenses incurred, so these are a liability.

Sales returns are a reduction in sales, so these are the opposite to income or a reduction in sales.

Prepaid income is income that has been prepaid by a customer so this is a liability to the business.

VAT owed to HMRC is money owed so this is a liability. Take care to note whether this is VAT owed **to** or **from** HMRC as VAT owed from HMRC is an asset.

Task 20 answer

You are working on the accounts for the year end **30 September 2019.**

You have been provided with the following information:

Accrual of motor expenses at 1 October 2018	£535
Prepayment of telephone expenses at 1 October 2018	£120
Prepayment of rental income at 1 October 2018	£1,200
Bank payments of motor expenses during the year	£6,600
Bank payments of telephone expenses during the year	£1,400
Rental income received during the year	£15,600

You are given the following information for the year-end adjustments:

The **bank payments** of **motor expenses** included insurance for the quarter ended **30 November 2019 of £333**. *Workings: This was included with the bank payments and includes the months of October and November which represents prepaid expenses of 2 months, so £333/3 and then multiplied by 2 months is £222. This is a prepaid expense.*

After the year end an invoice of **£240** for telephone expenses for the **quarter ended 31 October 2019** was received and paid. *Workings: This was received after the year end so was not included with the payments already made, so this must be an accrual. £240 was for the 3 months of August, September and October 2019 and two of these need to be added to the expenses as an accrued expense. £240/3 = £80 x 2 months = £160.*

Rental income is £1,200 per month for the full 12 months. *Workings: As you are told the rental income for the year this is the amount to transfer to the profit and loss and the balancing amount will represent prepaid income.*

You are required to prepare the motor expenses, telephone expenses and rental income accounts for the year ended 30 September clearly showing the amounts to be transferred to the statement of profit and loss.

Motor expenses

Debit	£	Credit	£
Bank (2)	6,600	Accrued expenses reversal (1)	535
		Prepaid expenses (3)	222
		Transfer to SoPL (4)	5,843
	6,600		6,600

Telephone expenses

Debit	£	Credit	£
Prepaid expenses reversal (1)	120		
Bank (2)	1,400		
Accrued expenses (3)	160	Transfer to SoPL (4)	1,680
	1,680		1,680

Rental income

Debit	£	Credit	£
Prepaid income (3)	2,400	Prepaid income reversal (1)	1,200
Transfer to SoPL (4)	14,400	Bank (cash book) (2)	15,600
	16,800		16,800

Task 21 – worked answer

You have been provided with the following information about a business with the year end of **31 March 2020**.

The balance on the rent income account at the beginning of the financial year was £300 and this represented a prepayment of rental income. **(Step 1)**

The cashbook shows receipts of rental income during the year of £3,800. **(Step 2)**

Included in the payments received was amount of £300 covering the period from 1 February 2020 to 30 April 2020. **(Step 3)** **(£300 covered 3 months to 30 April. The year end was March 2020, so April is prepaid for the next year)**

Calculate the rent income for the year ended 31 March 2020 to be transferred to the statement of profit and loss.

Answer: £4,000 (see workings in ledger account below)

Rent income

Debit	£	Credit	£
Prepaid income (3)	100	Prepaid income reversal (1)	300
		Bank (2)	3,800
Transfer to SoPL (4)	4,000		
	4,100		4,100

Task 22

You are working on the accounts of a business with the year end of 30 June 2020.

You are told that there is an opening prepayment on the insurance expense account of £500.

Bank payments made during the year for insurance expenses totalled £5,800.

Included in those payments were the following:

Van insurance	1 August 2019 – 31 July 2020	£480
Lorry insurance	1 November 2019 – 31 October 2020	£1,200

Complete the insurance account below, clearly showing the amount to be transferred to the statement of profit and loss.

Workings:

The van insurance covered 12 months including July 2020, which falls into the next financial year. £480 / 12 months = £40 prepaid for July.

The lorry insurance covered 12 months including July, August, September and October 2020, which fall into the next financial year. £1,200 / 12 months - £100. £100 x 4 months = £400.

The two prepayments added together are £440.

Insurance expenses

Debit	£	Credit	£
Prepaid expenses reversal (1)	500	Prepaid expenses (3)	440
Bank (2)	5,800		
		Transfer to SoPL (4)	5,860
	6,300		6,300

Prepaid expenses

Debit	£	Credit	£
Insurance expenses (3)	440		
		Bal c/d	440
	440		440
Bal b/d	440		

Task 23

TDJ Partnerships owns business premises and sublets one of its warehouses to another business for £120,000 a year. On the 1 January 2020 there was £20,000 of rent still owing. During the year ended 31 December 2020 £110,000 of rent payments were received.

Write up the rental income account for TDJ Partnership and the relevant accruals or prepayment account, balancing off the accounts appropriately.

Workings:

The rent owing at the start of the year was £20,000 so this is accrued income. This is reversed or brought down into the warehouse rent income account as a debit.

The bank payments received of £110,000 are credited to the income account (and debited to the bank account).

We were told that the rent for the year was £120,000 so this is the amount to be transferred to the SoPL.

The missing balancing figure if the accrued income of £30,000 which is credited to the income account and debited to the accrued income account.

Warehouse rent income

Debit	£	Credit	£
Accrued income reversal	20,000	Bank	110,000
Transfer to SoPL	120,000	Accrued income	30,000
	140,000		140,000

Accrued income

Debit	£	Credit	£
Warehouse rent income	30,000		
		Bal c/d	30,000
	30,000		30,000
Bal b/d	30,000		

Task 24:

TYL Manufacturing have a year end of 31 December. During the year to 31 December 2020 the following electricity bills were received and paid.

January, February and March £380

April, May and June   £450

July, August and September   £430

Write up the electricity account for the year based on this information.

Hint: You will need to estimate electricity costs based on usage through the year.

Note: The task has not asked for the accruals or prepayments account, but you might like to draw this to help you complete the task correctly.

Workings:

There was no opening accrual or prepayment, so there is no reversal for this task.

The year is from January 2020 to 31 December 2020 and electricity has been paid for from January through to the end of September. This means that we are missing October, November and December.

Add up the electricity costs for the year, i.e., the amount that has been paid. £380 + £450 + £430 = £1,260. This is the amount paid from the bank.

To estimate the accrual for the last 3 months we take the total paid for the first 9 months of the year and divide this by 9 and multiply by 3. £1,260 / 9 x 3 = £420. The is the accrued electricity expense for the year.

The electricity expenses is balanced with the transfer to the SoPL.

Electricity expenses

Debit	£	Credit	£
Bank	1,260		
Accrued expenses	420	Transfer to SoPL	1,680
	1,680		1,680

Accrued expenses

Debit	£	Credit	£
		Electricity expenses	420

Task 25

Enter the figures below into the correct debit or credit columns of the extract from the trial balance.

Ledger Account	Ledger Balance £	Debit £	Credit £
Prepaid expenses	360	**360**	
Accrued income	500	**500**	
Accrued expenses	800		**800**
Prepaid income	940		**940**

Prepaid expenses is a debit because it is an asset.

Accrued income is a debit because it is an asset.

Accrued expenses is a credit because it is a liability.

Prepaid income is a credit because it is a liability.

Task 26

The year end of a business is 31 March 2021. The balance on the prepaid expenses account at the start of the year was £300 and this represented prepaid insurance. Bank payments of £970 were made during the year. Included in that amount was a payment of £450 for the quarter ended 30 April 2021.

Complete the following sentences:

The balance on the insurance expense account at the start of the year was £**300**

The adjustment at the end of the year on the insurance expense account was

£**150** and this represented a ***prepaid expense***.

The amount of insurance expenses to be transferred to the statement of profit and loss

at the end of the year is £**1,120**.

<u>Workings</u>: The insurance payment included an amount of £450 for the quarter ended 30 April 2021. Because the year-end was March 2021, April was prepaid. £450 / 3 months = £150. This is a prepaid expense.

Insurance expenses

Debit	£	Credit	£
Prepaid expenses reversal	300	Prepaid expenses	150
Bank	970	Transfer to SoPL	1,120
	1,270		1,270

Chapter 7 – Quiz

1. A credit balance brought down at the start of the year on an expenses account represents which of the following?
a) Prepaid expense
b) Accrued expense

2. An adjustment for accrued expenses of £200 is added to the motor expenses account at the end of the year. What effect does this have on the profit for the year?
a) The profit increases.
b) The profit decreases.
c) There is no change to the profit.

3. Indicate whether the following will have a debit or credit balance.
a) Accrued income – *Debit / Credit*
b) Accrued expenses – *Debit / Credit*
c) Prepaid expenses – *Debit / Credit*
d) Prepaid income – *Debit / Credit*

4. Indicate whether the following statements are true or false.

	True	False
Prepaid expenses are carried down into the statement of financial position.		
Accrued income is carried down into the statement of profit and loss.		
Motor expenses is transferred to the statement of financial position.		
Office expenses is transferred to the statement of profit and loss.		
Prepaid income is a form of asset.		
Prepaid expenses are a form of income.		
Accrued expenses are a form of liability.		
Accrued income is a form of liability.		
Liabilities are shown in the statement of financial position.		
A reversal of a prepaid income will appear on the credit side of the income account.		

5. The accruals concept states that income and expenses are matched to when?
a) The period in which they were earned or incurred.
b) The period in which they were paid for.

6. To make an entry for a prepaid motor expense which accounts do you need to debit and credit?

a)	Dr Motor expenses	Cr Accrued expenses
b)	Dr Prepaid expenses	Cr Office expenses
c)	Dr Accrued expenses	Cr Motor expenses
d)	Dr Prepaid expenses	Cr Motor expenses

7. What would be the entries required in the prepaid income account and the commission income account to reverse a prepaid income of £100?

Dr_____ Cr _____

8. An adjustment for insurance expenses at the end of the year needs to be made. The year-end is 31 March 2021 and the final payment made on 1 February 2021 included a payment for premises insurance of £900 covering the period from 1 February 2021 to 30 April 2021.
Calculate the value of the adjustment required.

[   ]

9. Accrued expenses are shown as a *current liability / current asset* in the statement of financial position. Accrued income is shown as a *current liability / current asset* in the statement of financial position.

10. How confident are you with completing accruals and prepayments tasks now?

a) Very confident
b) Confident
c) Fairly confident
d) Need more practice

Quiz Answers

1. A credit balance brought down at the start of the year on an expenses account represents which of the following?
   c) Prepaid expense
   d) <u>Accrued expense</u>

2. An adjustment for accrued expenses of £200 is added to the motor expenses account at the end of the year. What effect does this have on the profit for the year?
   a) The profit increases.
   b) **<u>The profit decreases</u>**.
   c) There is no change to the profit.

(This is because the expenses have gone up so the profit goes down)

3. Indicate whether the following will have a debit or credit balance.
   e) Accrued income – ***<u>Debit</u>*** / *Credit*
   f) Accrued expenses – *Debit* / ***<u>Credit</u>***
   g) Prepaid expenses – ***<u>Debit</u>*** / *Credit*
   h) Prepaid income – *Debit* / ***<u>Credit</u>***

4. Indicate whether the following statements are true or false.

	True	False
Prepaid expenses are carried down into the statement of financial position.	√	
Accrued income is carried down into the statement of profit and loss.		√
Motor expenses is transferred to the statement of financial position.		√
Office expenses is transferred to the statement of profit and loss.	√	
Prepaid income is a form of asset.		√
Prepaid expenses are a form of income.	√	
Accrued expenses are a form of liability.	√	
Accrued income is a form of liability.		√
Liabilities are shown in the statement of financial position.	√	
A reversal of a prepaid income will appear on the credit side of the income account.		√

5. The accruals concept states that income and expenses are matched to when?
a) **<u>The period in which they were earned or incurred</u>**.
b) The period in which they were paid for.

6. To make an entry for a prepaid motor expense which accounts do you need to debit and credit?

a)	Dr Motor expenses	Cr Accrued expenses
b)	Dr Prepaid expenses	Cr Office expenses
c)	Dr Accrued expenses	Cr Motor expenses
d)	**Dr Prepaid expenses**	**Cr Motor expenses**

7. What would be the entries required in the prepaid income account and the commission income account to reverse a prepaid income of £100.

Dr Prepaid income £100

Cr Commission income £100

(Remember: To reverse the prepaid income, you must take it out of the prepaid income account as a debit and credit it to the commission income account).

8. An adjustment for insurance expenses at the end of the year needs to be made. The year-end is 31 March 2021 and the final payment made on 1 February 2021 included a payment for premises insurance of £900 covering the period from 1 February 2021 to 30 April 2021.

Calculate the value of the adjustment required.

> February, March and April were paid - £900
> April falls outside of the year as the year-end is 31 March.
> £900 / 3 months = **£300**

9. Accrued expenses are shown as a ***current liability*** / *current asset* in the statement of financial position. Accrued income is shown as a *current liability* / ***current asset*** in the statement of financial position.

(Remember: Accrued expenses are expenses that are still outstanding or owed at the end of the financial year. Accrued income is owed to the business at the end of the year).

10. How confident are you with completing accruals and prepayments tasks now?

a) Very confident
b) Confident
c) Fairly confident
d) Need more practice

I will leave you to answer this one! I do hope it is a) or b) !!

I hope that you have found this workbook useful. If you have any comments, you can find me on my Facebook page: Teresa Clarke AAT Tutoring.

Teresa Clarke FMAAT

Printed in Great Britain
by Amazon